PICTURE
PERFECT

PICTURE

Deco Photo Frames 1926-1946

PERFECT

Steve Starr

Photography by Mary Baber

This book is dedicated to the Starrs...and the stars.

First published in the United States of America in 1991
by Rizzoli International Publications, Inc.
300 Park Avenue South, New York, NY 10010

Library of Congress Cataloging-in-Publication Data

Starr, Steve.
Picture Perfect: deco photo frames, 1926–1946 / Steve Starr ;
photography by Mary Baber.
p. cm.
Includes bibliographical references (p. 155) and index.
ISBN 0-8478-1332-0
1. Picture frames and framing. 2. Decoration and ornament—
Art deco. I. Title.
N8550.S73 1991   91-14650
749'.7'09041—dc20   CIP

Designed by Charles Davey
Printed and bound by Dai Nippon, Tokyo, Japan

Front cover:
Circa 1930, geometric-style
frame silk-screened in turquoise,
ivory, and metallic silver on 1/8"-
thick glass. Mounted to an easel
back by chrome-plated steel
corner clips. Size: 10 x 12".
Window: 6 15/16 x 8 3/8".
Photo: Jean Harlow.

Back cover:
Top: Circa 1936, Streamlined-
style frame silk-screened in ivory,
black, and metallic gold on 1/8"-
thick glass. Mounted to an easel
back by brass corner clips.
Size: 8 x 10".
Window: 4 7/8 x 6 7/8".
Photo: Cary Grant.

Bottom: Circa 1946, romantic-
style frame with sandblasted leaf
design on 1/4"-thick, hand-
beveled glass. Mounted to an
easel back by nickel-plated
steel rosettes. Size: 14 x 17".
Window: 7 1/2 x 9 1/2".
Photo: Rita Hayworth.

Jacket photographs by
Mary Baber.
Author's photograph by
Steve Perry.

Page 1:
Circa 1937, Moderne-style
frame silk-screened in maroon,
taupe, and metallic gold on
1/8"-thick glass. Mounted to an
easel back by chrome-plated
steel corner clips. Size: 6 x 8".
Window: 3 x 4 1/2".
Photo: William Holden

Frontispiece:
Far left: Circa 1937, romantic-
style frame silk-screened in ivory,
accented with silver mirroring,
on 1/8"-thick glass. Mounted to
an easel back by chrome-plated
steel rosettes. Size: 10 x 12".
Oval window: 6 3/4 x 9 7/8".
Photo: Joan Blondell.

Center left: Circa 1942, patriotic-
theme frame silk-screened in
red, white, and blue on 1/8"-thick
glass. Mounted to an easel
back by chrome-plated steel
corner clips. Size: 8 x 10".
Window: 7 1/4 x 9 3/16".
Photo: Veronica Lake.

Center right: Circa 1941,
Streamlined-style frame silk-
screened in ivory, metallic
gold, and black on 1/8"-thick
glass. Mounted to an easel
back by nickel-plated steel
corner clips. Size: 8 x 10".
Window: 4 1/2 x 6 1/2".
Photo: Sonja Henie.

Far right: Circa 1938,
Moderne-style frame silk-screened
in black and metallic silver on
1/8"-thick glass. Held
on an easel back by a framing
of 5/16"-wide chrome-plated
steel. Size: 8 1/16 x 10 1/16".
Window: 4 5/8 x 6 5/8".
Photo: Pamela Nystul, a
performer in the 1972
"Vanity" production of Steve Starr
Studios. Photographed by
Robert Keeling.

Table of Contents

Left:
Steve (left), Gloria, and Adrienne
Starr in Miami Beach, Florida,
April 6, 1950. Photograph by
Roberta Starr.

Preface

When I was born on December 22, 1946, my family lived
in a beautiful two-bedroom apartment on Roscoe Street, just
off Lake Shore Drive on Chicago's north side. It was there
that I had my first glimpse of the Art Moderne style. Curved,
forest-green walls with streamlined moldings and indirect
lighting surrounded the modern furnishings. Chinese
sculptures and carvings accented the built-in display units.
We had the most modern of prewar appliances and fixtures,
as well as a spectacular yellow and jet-black bathroom.

Soon the fashionable apartment became too small for our
family of five. When my mother found an enormous ten-
room residence just up the street, she knew this was to be our
new home. But first she had to redecorate. Although the
world of decoration and design was about to enter a whole
new era of materials and shapes, the atomic age had not
met Gloria Starr.

In 1948, the big place was transformed into a glittering
showplace, a temple of 1940s glamour. Upon entering the
apartment, a guest would first notice the foyer walls, which
were papered in a design featuring metallic gold clouds
floating against a chocolate-brown background. A galaxy of
small white stars splashed through each cloud, and in the
center of each miniature Milky Way pranced a pale coral
unicorn. Straight ahead, through the doorway, one was
greeted by a love seat with tall, winglike arms. It was fully
upholstered in smooth white leather and stood between two
white Roman columns. White plaster console tables shaped
like giant scallop shells flanked the entry door.

Fascinating shapes and colors were found throughout the
apartment. Sultry, floral-print draperies covered the walls
and bays of the huge living room, where a painting of two
elegant zebras leaping through a silver jungle hung above a
gleaming mahogany piano. In the dining room, the sleek,

satinwood table surrounded by white leather wing chairs and a sideboard with rounded corners were reflected in a gigantic mirror. The four spacious bedrooms were approached via the forty-foot-long hall papered in a design of tiny metallic gold squares. The master bedroom was painted in a rich forest green, enhancing the burled maple and mahogany dressers. A mirrored, five-foot-long shadow box hung on one wall. Near each corner of the box was a clear glass shelf on which several crystal cologne bottles appeared to float. Below the shadow box was a large mirrored vanity table with beveled glass drawer pulls. When I was a child, I would crawl underneath the vanity, sit between the mirrors, and see my image infinitely repeated.

The aesthetic of that apartment was one important influence on my taste throughout the years.

Each year until I was eight, Ma, Dad, my two sisters, and I escaped Chicago's harsh winters for romantic Miami Beach. We always stayed in what is now known as the Art Deco District. For four months each year I played in the sun among the palm trees and streamlined buildings, most of them painted a glistening white. These wonderful structures had porthole windows with etched glass flamingos, terrazzo floors, glass brick walls, rounded balconies, and neon-lit lobbies glowing against Florida's clear evening sky.

In Miami Beach, I visited the gardens of the Spanish-style Roney Plaza Hotel, where an ancient talking parrot lived, and ogled the lobbies of the Saxony and the Sans Souci hotels. I explored the white beaches along Ocean Drive. One week I spent my time collecting postcards from every hotel along Collins Avenue. While I did attend school in Miami Beach, it took a back seat to all my other activities and explorations.

My surroundings in Florida forever influenced my design sense as well. In fact, one might say that I have devoted a good portion of my professional life to the celebration of twentieth-century art and design.

In 1967, I was 20 years old and in my second year of studies at the Chicago Academy of Fine Arts. My poster paintings of "mod" 1960s women were exhibited in many art shows, and my success with them had enabled me to open a shop, Steve Starr Studios. My store was wildly eclectic at first, and offered all manner of late–1960s jewelry, lamps, pedestals, statues, and my own line of three-

Above:
Adrienne (left), Gloria, and Roberta Starr in the family's Chicago apartment in 1947. A "modern" drapery fabric appears in the background.

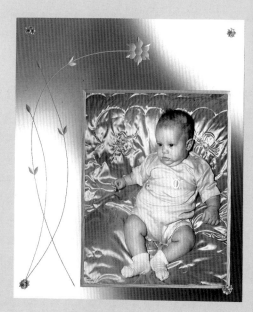

Above:
Steve Starr in 1947.

foot-square floor pillows and antique fabrics. I found myself drawn more and more to the past and began to offer mainly antiques and Art Deco items.

Soon I discovered and came to appreciate the fine craftsmanship of vintage clothing. The studio became known in the Chicago area as the source for the most beautiful day and evening wear from the past. Even *U.S. News and World Report* did a feature on the phenomenon, which included my own theories about the appeal of fashions from the past.

My interest in vintage clothing led me to become involved with theatrical productions. In 1970, I wrote, produced, directed, and costumed the first of five annual fall musical revues called "Vanity," which were held in Chicago's Athenaeum Theater. These productions were a showcase for the most spectacular pieces in my apparel collection. Many of the costumes were once owned or worn by famous people, including Jean Harlow, Sonja Henie, Elizabeth Taylor, Tiger Morse, and Edith Rockefeller McCormick. There were also famous designer names among the clothes and jewelry: Schiaparelli, Chanel, Miriam Haskell, Hobé, Trifari, and Hattie Carnegie. The "Vanity" productions featured sets decorated with vintage Art Deco and other period furnishings. The shows were a great success; thousands of Chicagoans attended them. The popularity of the shows indicated to me that when it came to the past people seemed to have unlimited curiosity.

In 1973, Chicago's first exhibition of Art Deco and Moderne objects and furnishings was held in both the Bergman Gallery and the Renaissance Society. I designed the layout and room settings at the gallery. For the opening day, six "Vanity" performers were dressed in the finest of period outfits and appeared to be "living" in the room settings. The appeal of the Art Deco style was realized at these exhibitions. Most people at the time had not seen original pieces from the period. There was a "skyscraper" dining-room suite of maple trimmed with black lacquer and upholstered in red leather, designed by Abel Faidy in 1927 for a Chicago penthouse. Vases of deeply etched crystal by Lalique, a bronze and marble table by Edgar Brandt, a desk and chair by Maurice Dufréne, and fabrics designed by Paul Poiret were also among the exhibition's displayed items. The Art Institute of Chicago lent a pony skin chaise longue by Le Corbusier and a side chair by Jacques-Emile Ruhlmann.

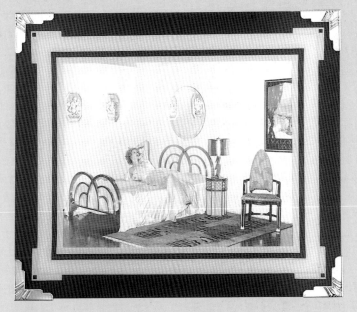

Above:
"Vanity" performer Jan Poss relaxes in a room setting executed by Steve Starr for the first Art Deco exhibition in Chicago, at the Bergman Gallery. Photograph by Bob Bishop.

Below:
The wall of frames at Steve Starr Studios, Chicago, Illinois. Photograph by Jim Hedrich, Hedrich/Blessing, Chicago. Reprinted by permission of *Metropolitan Home*.

Along one wall of the gallery, displayed on pedestals, was a collection of dazzling Bakelite and Catalin radios in a rainbow of brilliant colors. Also on display was a highly coveted 1936 Spartan "Bluebird" radio encased in blue mirrored glass trimmed with chrome. In another case, I exhibited my own collection of crystal cologne bottles by Verlys, Lalique, and Baccarat, among others. A section of the exhibition was devoted to jewelry made of Bakelite, enamel, silver, and crystal. Standing behind some enameled cigarette and makeup cases were three glass photo frames. They were silk-screened in black and ivory. The beauty of these frames stuck in my mind.

I hired a photographer to take some pictures of the exhibition. These photos, along with other publicity photographs, personal photos, photos from "Vanity" reviews, and photographs of some of the famous people who had visited my studio—Bette Midler, Diana Ross, and Patti LaBelle, among others—had really begun to accumulate. Many of the photographs had been taken by well-known Chicago photographers such as Victor Skrebneski, David Puffer, and Robert Keeling. I wanted to display these photos, but I wasn't sure how.

In 1976, I decided to redecorate the store. The copper-colored, geometric-patterned 1920s satin draperies that hung on one wall were beginning to look their age. In their place I hung a leaf-patterned wallpaper in natural tones, and I covered the remaining walls in a neutral grasscloth paper. Suddenly the high-ceilinged room looked naked for the first time, but I dismissed the idea of covering the walls with merchandise for sale. I owned one Art Deco–style frame, similar to the ones I'd seen at the exhibition. I had used it in the store to display the studio's business hours in the front window. This frame was silk-screened in a design of maroon, ivory, and metallic silver. I took it out of the window, inserted a "Vanity" photo, and hung it on the grasscloth wall. It looked great, but lonely. I knew I needed more frames. Impossible, I thought. How many of these frames were still around?

I began searching for more frames. Everywhere I went, in every city I visited, from San Francisco to New York to Miami, I looked for frames. I went to antique shops, garage sales, house sales, and resale shops. Each time I bought one I thought I had probably seen them all. But I kept on

Above:
Superstar Diana Ross visited Steve Starr Studios in 1975, one of several celebrities drawn to the vintage items on display. Her portrait hangs in one of the hundreds of frames Starr has amassed. Photograph by Steve Starr.

searching. I felt possessed!

In three years an entire wall measuring 20 feet long and 14 feet high was completely covered with over 250 photo frames. Their color and pattern variety astonished clients. I had finally found a way to showcase my collection of photographs and decorate the studio.

I continued to sell original Art Deco and Moderne furnishings and accessories. And I continued to collect frames. Soon the remaining walls of my shop were completely covered by frames. I had amassed a collection of over 600 frames dating from the 1920s to the 1940s.

Through word of mouth and newspaper and magazine stories about my shop and its collections, my studio became known all over the United States and in many European cities. Visitors came from all over to shop and to admire my collection of frames. The "oohs" and "ahs" of the frame admirers were, and are, always fun to hear. I realized, though, that there were many visitors to the studio who were very disappointed when they found out that the frames were not for sale.

Recently I realized that my collection, though certain to be in a museum one day, deserved to be seen by a larger audience. Even though thousands of people had viewed them in the studio, I wanted to share their beauty and variety with others. The best way to accomplish this, I felt, was to photograph the frames with the most unusual motifs and beautiful designs, and those with the rarest color schemes, and present them in a book.

When these frames were originally sold, they often contained photographs of movie stars. For this book, I felt that it was most appropriate to present these frames with movie star photographs in them. The Hollywood studios, particularly Paramount, Universal, Metro-Goldwyn-Mayer, and Twentieth Century Fox, promoted their stars with thousands of stock publicity photos. Frame manufacturers filled their frames with these glamorous images. Many of the frames I purchased still had these star photographs in them. In the cases where original photos were missing, I was able to replace them with original publicity photos. I tried to match the photos to the date of the frame, and I also considered the style of the frame, attempting to find an aesthetically pleasing match in an existing publicity photograph. The old photographs I collected were found in

Above:
Sam Starr in a circa 1931 photograph. With the popularity of the camera increasing during the 1920s, 1930s, and 1940s, the deco-style frames produced provided hundreds of choices for those who wished to display precious family photographs.

antique shops and at stores and shows that specialize in antique and vintage movie memorabilia.

The glass-and-metal easel-backed photo frames I have collected are by no means the only types of frames produced in the United States from 1926 to 1946. There were frames made of Bakelite, Catalin, celluloid, marble, wood, clear acrylic, and other materials. My large collection consists only of glass and/or metal easel-backed frames, and I believe this makes it even more interesting as a collection. The variety of shapes, sizes, motifs, and colors of the frames in this collection is amazing, considering the production techniques employed to produce them and the reasonable prices originally assigned to them.

These particular frames reached their height of production in the 1920s, 1930s, and 1940s. I have attempted, through various methods of research, to give an approximate date for each frame in this book. In some cases, dates have been assigned through educated guesses. Some frames, especially those with patriotic motifs, were clearly produced during the World War II years; others are less clearly datable. New patterns were introduced every year, yet basic ideas and shapes changed gradually, and some patterns were sold unchanged for many years.

I continue to add to my own collection. My fascination with these frames is unending, as there is always a new discovery to be made.

Steve Starr

Introduction

Above:
Circa 1936, Moderne-style frame
silk-screened in cherry red,
accented with silver mirroring, on
$\frac{1}{8}$"-thick glass. Mounted to an
easel back with embossed steel
bands. Size: $2^{11}/_{16}$ X $3\frac{1}{2}$".
Window: $1\frac{1}{2}$ X $1\frac{3}{4}$".
Photo: Duke Ellington.

The glass-and-metal photograph frames designed and manufactured in the years from 1926 to 1946 were not high-design objects. They were manufactured mostly by small firms throughout the United States and sold in department stores, five-and-dimes, and photographic studios at affordable prices. Places as varied as Tiffany & Company, Marshall Field & Company, W.T. Grant, Kresge's, and Woolworth's sold this type of frame. The fancier the design of the frame, the "better" the original retail outlet. Most were manufactured in now-anonymous studios and manufacturing firms from Los Angeles to Boston. Some of the manufacturers of the frames can be identified: metal frames sometimes were stamped with the producer's name, but most were either never marked or marked with an adhesive-backed label which has not survived the years of wear. Most of the designers of the frames are unknown and, if they are known, they are not "famous." A large number of these craftspeople produced their own lines at home or in small studios and sold them directly to the retail establishments.

Two important events helped to shape the aesthetics and the choice of medium in the manufacture of these consumer products. While there had always been frames for photographs, beginning with the small, leatherbound Daguerreotype cases of the mid-nineteenth century, continuing through to the present day, it was the development of an enormously easier method for the production of plate glass by the Pittsburgh Plate Glass Company in 1928 which contributed to the glass frame's success. The "Pittsburgh Process" speeded production, improved quality, and minimized the waves and imperfections previously found in sheet glass. The technological development allowed for the construction of a clear, mostly glass frame, consisting of a sheet of glass attached to a cardboard or wooden easel with some kind of metal attaching element. It was the simplicity of such a construction, without the heaviness of a literal framing of wood or another material holding the backing and glass together, which enabled manufacturers to produce attractive frames—embellished with silk-screened images on the face of the glass—at a reasonable price. (Prices were not standard, but some frames could be purchased for as little as a dime.)

The aesthetic adopted for the decoration of these frames was influenced by a major exposition in 1925 in Paris celebrating modern design and introducing many "new" decorative motifs (World War I had delayed the exposition, so many of the styles presented were not so avant-garde: Bauhaus ideas were not part of the exposition's displays, due to the anti-German sentiment in France at the time). The "Exposition Internationale des Artes Décoratifs et Industrieles Modernes" introduced to the world a concept or style of design later referred to by the pared-down term Art Deco (which was actually coined in the 1960s). It brought to worldwide attention a new formal aesthetic, very different from the previous Victorian taste for excess and the rustic appearance of Arts and Crafts Movement objects. Visitors from many nations, the United States included, found a strong attraction to new, modern, stylized forms exhibited. These forms seemed to embody what the twentieth century "should" look like.

The 1925 exhibition was conceived during a time of great prosperity. Luxuriously crafted objects, incorporating some of the rarest and most exotic materials on earth, were displayed. Zebrawood, Macassar, ebony, shagreen, ivory, tortoiseshell, and bronze were only some of the choice materials used in the designs for household items and furnishings. The "decoration" of these objects often incorporated the sophisticated, stylized motifs now associated with the era: elegant borzois, gazelles, and peacocks, fountains, and varied interpretations of floral subjects, among many others. The most famous European designers of the day created some of the richest furnishings the world had ever seen, intended for use by the wealthiest people on the globe.

This new design style from Europe appealed to machine-age Americans. Manufacturers sensed it and, in a version of the "trickle-down effect," they began to apply the Art Deco

Below:
Circa 1932, geometric-style frame silk-screened in black, accented with silver mirroring, on ⅛"-thick glass. Mounted to an easel back by nickel-plated steel rosettes. Size: 10 x 12". Window: 6¾ x 8¾". Photo: Joan Crawford.

Opposite, top:
Circa 1938, Moderne-style frame silk-screened in ivory and maroon, with clear areas, on ⅛"-thick glass, backed by a textured foil mat. Mounted to an easel back by chrome-plated steel corner clips. Size: 8 x 10". Window: 4¾ x 6³⁄₁₆". Photo: Jean Arthur.

Opposite, bottom:
Circa 1931, Moderne-style frame silk-screened in ivory, cinnabar red, and metallic silver on ⅛"-thick glass. Mounted to an easel back by chrome-plated steel corner clips. Size: 10 x 12". Arched window: 7⅛ x 9⅛". Photo: Ramon Novarro.

motifs to even the most mundane of household objects. Before long, zigzags and other geometric patterns, stylized flowers, fluid nude figures, lightning bolts, and sun rays found their way onto hundreds of consumer products, including cologne bottles, desk sets, radios, clocks, lamps, vases, makeup and cigarette cases, pottery, and cameras. The designers of photo frames were among those who adopted the new "Jazz Age" aesthetic. The ease with which a silk-screen could be made in order to apply a design to glass made the frames perhaps the most changeable, market-responsive, and varied market for the new Art Deco style. In many cases, the silk-screened designs on the frames mimicked the luxurious textures of the materials employed in original Art Deco designs.

As the twenties became the thirties and the Great Depression occurred, a cleaner aesthetic emerged, derived from the fluidity of the lines in purely Art Deco motifs. The design elements adopted during the 1920s perhaps reminded people too much of the frivolity of that era.

The ideal of modernism in the 1930s was represented by clean, simple shapes and lines, and in pure colors and contrasts. The Moderne style was created using newer materials such as aluminum, rayon, and plastics. The new methods for producing glass made its use particularly appealing to designers. Glass block, for instance, emerged as an important style element in American houses of the 1930s. The Moderne look was often represented by three parallel lines drawn vertically or horizontally across the surface of an object. This decorative motif was applied to the design of everything from washing machines to apartment buildings and, of course, photo frames.

The most popular symbol of the 1930s, however, was a straight line ending in a curve: the "streamline." The most famous and influential industrial designers of the day, such as Walter Dorwin Teague, Raymond Loewy, Lurell Guild, and Russel Wright, among others, advocated the Streamlined style, as it came to be known. Americans embraced this style, and it became quite popular. Streamlined designs appeared on many things during the 1930s and 1940s, from planes and trains to vacuum cleaners and pencil sharpeners to furniture, household objects, and photo frames.

Designs were always made to be saleable and

decoratively appealing to a wide group of buyers. Therefore, while the general design trends of an era are reflected, there was also the need to appeal to the wide market with pretty, romantic designs, appealing not only to "modern" tastes but to those consumers who merely wanted a decorative object, not a design statement. This accounts for the wide popularity of floral motifs in these frames, applied throughout the decades. With the onset of the Second World War in the 1940s, frame manufacturers responded to the patriotism of many Americans whose family members served in the war effort, adopting the red, white, and blue of the American flag as a design motif, and often creating a border of tricolored bunting, stars, the flag itself, or even the figures of marching soldiers surrounding the portrait display area. The ease with which a design could be produced, merely requiring a new silk-screen to be created, allowed frame designers and manufacturers to respond immediately to market demands.

The specifics of the construction and design of these frames remained unchanged over the decades. In all cases, a sheet of glass, usually ⅛-to-¼-inch thick, was cut to a desired size. This sheet of glass, called the face, was bordered with silk-screened, hand-painted, hand-engraved, or hand-etched designs. In some cases designs were sandblasted onto the glass. This decorative border surrounds a central display area, left clear so that a photograph can be seen behind the glass. This area for the display of the photograph is called the window.

Some frame faces were silk-screened with an all-over design, where the colors and patterns selected for the design made the glass areas surrounding the photo display area opaque. Other frame designs took advantage of the clear properties of glass, printing the design selectively to allow for clear areas to remain and a paper mat, usually of metallic silver foil, behind the glass to show through, adding a three-dimensional effect to the overall frame design.

Tinted glass was also used. Cobalt blue, peach-colored, and gold glass were adopted. A black-and-white photograph would acquire a pleasant tint when it was displayed behind such glass. On some frames, strips of colored glass, sometimes mirrored, were attached to the edges of a clear glass face. This second layer of glass was attached to the frame body with either glue, decorative

Below:
Circa 1943, patriotic-theme frame silk-screened in ivory, black, and metallic gold on ⅛"-thick glass. Mounted to an easel back by chrome-plated steel corner clips. Size: 9 x 11".
Window: 6¼ x 8¼".
Photo: David Niven.

Opposite, top:
Circa 1942, Moderne-style frame silk-screened in ivory and maroon, accented with silver mirroring, on ⅛"-thick glass. Mounted to an easel back by nickel-plated steel corner clips. Size: 8 x 10".
Window: 5 x 7".
Photo: Fred MacMurray.

Opposite, bottom:
Circa 1934, geometric-style frame silk-screened in ivory and black on ⅛"-thick glass. Held on an easel back by a framing of 7/16"-wide chrome-plated steel. Size: 5⅞ x 7⅞".
Window: 5⁵/₁₆ x 3⁹/₁₆".
Photo: Cesar Romero.

corner clips, or metal brackets.

Other methods for enhancing the clear sheet of glass include engraving, scalloping, and mirroring. An engraved design could be left naturally frosted or polished clear, depending on the desired effect, adding another dimension to the design. Scalloping required the use of a chipping tool to create a curved edge. Generally, a thicker face was used for both decorative applications. Mirror accenting required the entire surface of the glass to be mirrored, either in silver or, in some rarer cases, gold. A protective coating was then applied to the areas which were to remain mirrored in the finished product. When the coating dried, the remaining areas of unprotected mirroring were washed away. Then, if desired, other colors could be screened onto the glass over and behind the mirroring.

After a glass design was determined, it was ready to be attached to an easel back of cardboard or wood. Frame faces were attached to easels in various ways. One of the more traditional methods was with a thin framing of brass, often embossed with a decorative design as well. A more "modern" look was achieved through the use of a thin framing of nickel- or chrome-plated steel or brass.

The use of corner clips was perhaps the most popular method for attaching glass to backing. Most often made of steel and then nickel- or chrome-plated, and sometimes made of brass, the clips were usually embossed with some kind of design, contributing to the overall design of a frame. Clips, aside from their purpose of attaching glass to backing, also provided protection from chipping or breaking at the corners of the frame. While most were made of metal, a small number of the clips made were crafted of a thick paper with embossed or printed designs on them. Corner clips are generally not a good indicator of a frame's age. However, the fancier embossed corner-clip designs one often finds were most likely created during the 1920s and early 1930s.

Another common means for easel mounting was with screws. Holes drilled near the four corners of the glass accommodated the screws, which were held in place by small bolts. These screws often had a decorative head resembling a flower, commonly known as a rosette. Rosette screws were made of nickel-, chrome-, or brass-plated steel. Occasionally a backplate was used behind the rosette for added decoration and protection. Backplates were usually

round or square and embossed or plated to complement the rosette. Some rosette screws were given smooth or star-shaped glass or plastic heads as well. The rosette screws produced during the period did not change much from the 1920s to the 1940s, so they too do not offer a good indication of a frame's age. Screws with clear and smooth glass heads, however, were probably produced in the late 1930s and early 1940s.

On smaller frames another method of attachment was sometimes used. Four bands of polished aluminum or plated steel were attached to an easel back, one near each corner. The bands were bent and wrapped approximately ¼ inch over the edge of the glass face. Rounded at the edges, the bands were often embossed with a simple design.

The cleanest connection between glass and easel backing occurred when the two were glued together. The flat surface of the glass was retained, and the frame was lighter in general. This type of mounting, however, can cause problems as years go by, as the glue disintegrates in areas, sometimes taking the silk-screened design with it.

Cardboard was by far the first choice of material for American-made easel backs during the 1920s, 1930s, and 1940s. The cardboard was usually embossed with a texture or pattern or covered with a fabric of some kind, usually velvet. Wood was rarely used as a backing. In general, the decoration of the easel backs was more complex in the 1920s and early 1930s, with swirling floral designs often chosen. The patterns of the easel backs from the mid-1930s and later tend to be more simple. However, easel back designs were continued for years, so they are not a foolproof indicator of frame dates. An exception is the cleverly designed, self-locking easel stand, named the "Turnit," found on some frames. This device was not marketed until 1935.

Dating Frames

If you are considering the purchase of a vintage frame and are unsure if it is an original, keep the following information in mind.

Sometimes frames are in exceedingly good condition. They must have been well taken care of in a good climate that did not deteriorate the paint, glue, or silver mirroring. Check the turnbuttons on the back of the frame that keep the easel "door" closed. If they are embossed, the frame probably dates from the 1920s or early 1930s. Most newer frames do not have this detail. Also check the easel back to see if there is an elaborate pattern on it, particularly a floral pattern, the preferred pattern on earlier easel backs of the 1920s and 1930s.

Examine the hardware of the frame. The fancier the corner clip and rosette screw design, the older the frame, in most cases. Glass-headed screws also indicate that the frame is an original. This type of screw has not been used on a reproduction frame.

Also look at the glass details. If any engraving exists, the frame is probably a period piece. Any beveling done on a curved edge would also most likely indicate an original design. Frames with colored glass and those trimmed with colored mirroring were probably created during the 1930s or 1940s.

One of the best ways to determine if a frame is a vintage 1920s, 1930s, or 1940s specimen is by the size of its window. Window areas vary in size, often with measurements that seem strange to contemporary eyes. Window areas were geared to the popular sizes of photographic prints of the day, just as today's frames are geared to 3 x 5-, 5 x 7-, and 8 x 10-inch prints. A popular film of the day, size 122, was in use from the 1920s to the early 1940s and produced postcard-size prints of 3¼ x 5½ inches. Kodak's Beau Brownie camera, which used 120 film, produced images measuring 2¼ x 3¼ inches. For smaller frames, designed for the purpose of snapshot display, the window areas were usually made to accommodate the film print sizes.

Perhaps the best advice of all is to purchase a frame from a reliable dealer or shop. Though few people know much about these frames, authenticity can be determined from the provenance of the frame, which the dealer should be able to supply upon request.

Opposite:
Corner clips, used to attach glass to an easel back, were created in a variety of finishes, shapes, and embossed patterns.

Frame Care

Decades of dirt can scar the beauty of vintage frames. Here are some tips for keeping frames in good shape.

Carefully take the frame apart. Stubborn rosette screws usually can be removed after the application of a small amount of a lubricant such as WD-40. In most cases, corner clips can be gently pulled off the glass and backing, but if they have become fused to the frame one can remove them by placing the frame face down on a flat, cushioned surface and gently nudging the inner edge of the corner clip with a screwdriver, pushing outward very slowly. This should ease off the corner clips without damaging them. Always keep in mind, however, that if a piece of the glass is chipped, it is chipped permanently.

Remove paper foil mats in order to clean the glass beneath. Frames with a metal framing holding the face on the easel back must be handled carefully. On such frames, lift the small tab at one corner of the frame. When lifted, it will allow you to separate the framing: a single piece of metal scored, mitered, and bent at each corner. This allows one to clean both sides of the glass face. Be especially careful with the corner tab; if it breaks off there is no way to repair it correctly. On frames with faces that slide along a channel in the framing, the process of removal should be much easier.

To clean the face and to avoid the nightmare of removing the painted design along with the dirt, spray glass cleaner onto a cloth first and then very carefully attack the dirty glass, guiding the cloth within the clear areas. Dry dust the painted surface.

Polish corner clips and rosette screws gently with the finest grade of steel wool. A small dab of metal polish, such as Wenol, should bring back the metal's luster.

On some frames you may find that bits of paint have flaked off over the decades. With a tiny brush and the right color paint, one can restore the painted surface of a frame's face. Always test the paint on a piece of glass before applying it to the frame's glass, as colors often change as they dry on glass as opposed to paper. Black and ivory are the easiest colors to match, but it may take some time to find the perfect match for other colors.

When the cardboard easel back of a frame is broken or cracked, a new back can usually be purchased through a picture framing store. If only the easel stand is broken, it can be replaced with a new one, retaining the much-preferred original easel back.

When rosette screws and corner clips are missing, check with the most ancient hardware store in your vicinity and with antiques shops or resale shops. If you are a serious collector, buy broken frames for their hardware, if it is in good condition, and use it on a frame with pieces missing. Some people (purists) might find this kind of mixing and matching distasteful. It is my feeling, however, that if restoration is necessary in order to use an old frame, it is worth it.

These frames should be used. Permanently changing the character of any original piece is not advocated, but repairing and cleaning it can only enhance its beauty.

Above:
A turnbutton used on some frames from the early 1930s.

Above:
Labels identifying the makers and/or sellers of these vintage frames are a rare find.

Below:
The Kodak Beau Brownie camera of 1930. Frame windows often were sized to accommodate the prints that mass-market cameras produced. Reprinted courtesy of Eastman Kodak Company, © Eastman Kodak Company.

Opposite, top:
An example of a cardboard easel back with corner clips attached. The frame back shown is a circa 1936 design.

Opposite, bottom:
The self-locking easel stand is found on frames created after the mid-1930s.

ROMANTIC

What better way to display the portrait of a loved one or a beloved film star than in a lushly detailed, elegant, and charmingly patterned frame? The Romantic-style frame was embellished with floral themes, animal motifs, ribbons and bows, tassels, and other "pretty" elements. This type of design was perhaps the most popular during the 1920s, 1930s, and 1940s.

Opposite:
Circa 1935. Silk-screened in ivory and black on 1/8"-thick glass. Held on an easel back by a framing of 3/8"-wide chrome-plated steel. Size: 10 1/8 x 12 3/16". Window: 7 1/2 x 9 9/16". Photo: Paulette Goddard.

Above:
Circa 1926. Hand-engraved and mirrored 1/8"-thick glass. Mounted to an easel back by nickel-plated steel rosettes. Size: 3 1/2 x 4 3/4". Window: 1 15/16 x 2 15/16". Photo: Alice White.

Opposite:
Circa 1928. Silk-screened in black, cream, and metallic gold on 1/8"-thick glass. Mounted to an easel back by chrome-plated brass corner clips. Size: 8 x 10". Window: 5 3/16 x 7 3/16".
Photo: Norma Talmadge.

Below:
Circa 1933. Silk-screened in black, ivory, and metallic gold on 1/8"-thick glass. Mounted to an easel back by chrome-plated steel corner clips. Size: 10 x 12". Window: 6 1/4 x 8 1/4".
Photo: Gilbert Roland.

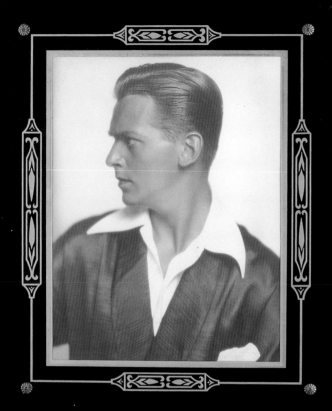

Left:
Circa 1932. Silk-screened in black and accented with gold on ⅛"-thick glass. Mounted to an easel back by brass-plated steel rosettes. Size: 10 x 12". Window: 6⅞ x 8⅞".
Photo: Douglas Fairbanks, Jr.

Below:
Circa 1926. Silk-screened in black and metallic gold on ⅛"-thick glass. Mounted to an easel back by brass corner clips. Size: 6 x 8". Arched window: 3⁷⁄₁₆ x 4¹⁵⁄₁₆".
Photo: Vilma Banky.

Opposite:
Circa 1930. Hand-beveled and-engraved ¼"-thick glass, mirrored with 24-karat gold. Mounted to an easel back by nickel-plated steel rosettes. Size: 8⅞ x 11⅝". Window: 4⅝ x 6⅝".
Photo: Barbara La Marr.

Below:
Circa 1928. Silk-screened in
ivory, black, and metallic gold
on ⅛"-thick glass. Mounted to
an easel back by chrome-plated
steel corner clips. Size: 8 x 10".
Window: 4³/₁₆ x 6³/₁₆".
Photo: Greta Garbo.

Below:
Circa 1928. Silk-screened in
black, ivory, and metallic gold
on ⅛"-thick glass. Mounted to
an easel back by embossed,
chrome-plated steel corner
clips. Size: 8 x 10".
Window: 4³/₁₆ x 6³/₁₆".
Photo: John Gilbert.

Opposite:
Circa 1926. Silk-screened in
ivory, maroon, and metallic gold
on ⅛"-thick glass. Mounted to an
easel back with chrome-plated
steel corner clips. Size: 10 x 12".
Window: 6³/₁₆ x 8³/₁₆".
Photo: Rudolph Valentino.

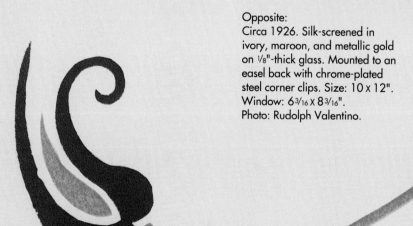

Rodolphe Valentino

Below:
Circa 1928. Egyptian-style design, silk-screened in green, violet, and jet black on ⅛"-thick glass. Mounted to an easel back by nickel-plated steel rosettes. Size: 9⅞ x 12".
Window: 6½ x 8½".
Photo: Lupe Velez.

Below:
Circa 1931. Silk-screened in black, mint green, and ivory on ⅛"-thick glass. Mounted to an easel back by nickel-plated steel corner clips. Size: 5½ x 6½".
Window: 2¾ x 3¾".
Photo: Colleen Moore.

Above:
Circa 1928. Framing of chrome-plated brass, 1⁵⁄₁₆" wide, accented with a brushed chrome design, and silk-screened in black and orange. Size: 9 x 11".
Window: 6³⁄₈ x 8¹⁄₄".
Photo: Constance Talmadge.

Above:
Circa 1928. Framing of chrome-plated brass, 1¹⁄₄" wide, with a brushed chrome design, accented with silk-screened black and red lacquer flowers. Size: 9 x 11".
Window: 6³⁄₈ x 8¹⁄₄".
Photo: Clara Bow.

Left:
Circa 1926. Silk-screened in ivory, black, and metallic silver on 1/8"-thick glass. Held on an easel back by a framing of nickel-plated steel. Size: 8 x 10½". Window: 5⁵/₁₆ x 7³/₈". Photo: Gilda Gray.

Left:
Circa 1937. Silk-screened in ivory, black, and metallic gold on 1/8"-thick glass. Held on an easel back by a framing of ⁵/₁₆"-wide brass. Size: 9⅛ x 11¹/₁₆". Window: 7½ x 8½". Photo: Rosemary Lane.

Opposite:
Circa 1927. Mirrored, hand-engraved, and hand-beveled ¼"-thick glass. Mounted to a wood easel back by glass-headed rosette screws. Made in France. Size: 10 x 14¼". Window: 6³/₄ x 8³/₈". Photo: Thelma Todd.

Below:
Circa 1937. Silk-screened in
blue, black, and metallic gold
on ⅛"-thick glass. Mounted to
an easel back by brass corner
clips. Size: 4 x 5".
Window: 1⅞ x 2⅞".
Photo: Olivia DeHavilland.

Below:
Circa 1937. Silk-screened in
cherry red, cream, and metallic
gold on ⅛"-thick glass. Mounted
to an easel back by brass corner
clips. Size: 4 x 5".
Window: 1⅞ x 2⅞".
Photo: Loretta Young.

Opposite:
Circa 1934. Silk-screened in
black, ivory, and metallic gold
on ⅛"-thick glass. Mounted to
an easel back by chrome-plated
steel corner clips. Size: 11 x 13".
Window: 7³⁄₁₆ x 9³⁄₁₆".
Photo: Dolores Del Rio.

Right:
Circa 1936. Silk-screened in
black, ivory, and metallic gold
on ⅛"-thick glass. Mounted to
an easel back by chrome-plated
steel corner clips. Size: 11 x 13".
Window: 7½ x 9¼".
Photo: Greta Garbo.

Right:
Circa 1942. Silk-screened in
black, metallic gold, and ivory
on ⅛"-thick glass. Mounted to
an easel back by solid brass
corner clips. Size: 9⅞ x 12".
Window: 6½ x 8½".
Photo: Lena Horne.

Opposite:
Circa 1937. Silk-screened in
black and ivory, accented with
silver mirroring, on ⅛"-thick
glass. Mounted to an easel
back by nickel-plated steel
rosettes. Size: 10 x 12".
Window: 8¹⁵⁄₁₆ x 7".
Photo: Dorothy Lamour.

Opposite, top left:
Circa 1936. Silk-screened in
ivory and metallic gold on
1/8"-thick glass. Mounted to an
easel back by nickel-plated
brass corner clips. Size: 10 x 12".
Window: 7 1/8 X 9 1/8".
Photo: Rochelle Hudson.

Opposite, top right:
Circa 1930. Silk-screened in
ivory, black, and metallic gold
on 1/8"-thick glass. Mounted to
an easel back by brass-plated
steel corner clips. Size: 4 1/2 x 5 1/2".
Window: 2 7/8 x 3 7/8".
Photo: Lila Lee.

Opposite, bottom left:
Circa 1932. Silk-screened in
black and metallic gold, accented
with silver mirroring, on 1/8"-thick
glass. Held on an easel back by
a framing of 3/16"-wide brass.
Size:10 1/8 X 12 1/8".
Window: 6 1/8 x 8 3/16".
Photo: Zasu Pitts.

Opposite, bottom right:
Circa 1935. Silk-screened in
maroon, ivory, and metallic silver
on 1/8"-thick glass. Mounted to
an easel back by chrome-plated
steel corner clips. Size: 8 x 10".
Window: 4 5/8 x 6 1/8".
Photo: Mary Carlisle.

Above:
Circa 1933. Silk-screened in
crystallized metallic silver and
black, accented with a hand-
engraved, metallic gold painted
design, on 1/8"-thick glass.
Mounted to an easel back by
nickel-plated steel. Size: 11 x 13".
Oval window: 7 1/2 x 9 1/2".
Photo: Ruby Keeler and
Dick Powell.

Above:
Circa 1937. Silk-screened in black and metallic silver, accented with silver mirroring, on ¼"-thick glass with a hand-tooled scalloped edge. Mounted to an easel back by nickel-plated steel rosettes.
Size: 11 x 13".
Window: 6¾ x 8¾".
Photo: William Powell.

Above:
Circa 1937. Silk-screened in ivory and metallic silver, accented with silver mirroring, on ¼"-thick glass with a hand-tooled scalloped edge. Mounted to an easel back by nickel-plated steel rosettes. Size: 11 x 13".
Window: 6¾ x 8¾".
Photo: Myrna Loy.

Below:
Circa 1930. Silk-screened in
ivory, black, and metallic gold
on ⅛"-thick glass. Mounted to
an easel back by nickel-plated
corner clips. Size: 4 x 5".
Window: 2 x 5".
Photo: Nils Asther.

Below:
Circa 1934. Silk-screened in
ivory and black on ⅛"-thick glass.
Held on an easel back by a
framing of ⅜"-wide chrome-
plated steel. Size: 10¹/₁₆ X 12⅛".
Window: 7 x 9".
Photo: Ruth Chatterton.

Left:
Circa 1936. Silk-screened in ivory, black, and metallic gold on ⅛"-thick glass. Mounted to an easel back by brass-plated steel corner clips. Size: 3½ x 4½". Window: 1⅞ x 2⅞".
Photo: Olympe Bradna.

Left:
Circa 1936. Silk-screened in salmon, ivory, and metallic gold on ⅛"-thick glass. Mounted to an easel back by polished steel corner clips. Size: 3 x 4". Window: 1⅜ x 1⅞".
Photo: Rosalind Russell.

Below:
Circa 1928. Silk-screened in
ivory and maroon, accented with
silver mirroring, on ⅛"-thick
glass. Mounted to an easel back
by nickel-plated steel corner
clips. Size: 8 x 10".
Window: 4¹¹/₁₆ X 6⁵/₈".
Photo: Billie Dove.

Overleaf left:
Circa 1935. Silk-screened in
cream and maroon, with clear
snowflake designs, on ⅛"-thick
glass. Backed by a textured
silver foil mat. Mounted to an
easel back by chrome-plated
steel corner clips. Size: 8 x 10".
Window: 4¾ x 6¾".
Photo: Frances Dee.

Overleaf right:
Circa 1932. Black, silver, and
gray design printed on a paper
mat behind ⅛"-thick glass. Held
on an easel back by a framing
of ⅜"-wide chrome-plated steel.
Size: 10 x 12".
Window: 6¹¹/₁₆ X 8¹³/₁₆".
Photo: Ken Meynard.

Ken Maynard -11

Left:
Circa 1938. Silk-screened in maroon, ivory, and metallic gold on ⅛"-thick glass. Mounted to an easel back by chrome-plated steel corner clips. Size: 11 x 13".
Window: 7⁵/₁₆ X 9⁵/₁₆".
Photo: William "Hopalong Cassidy" Boyd.

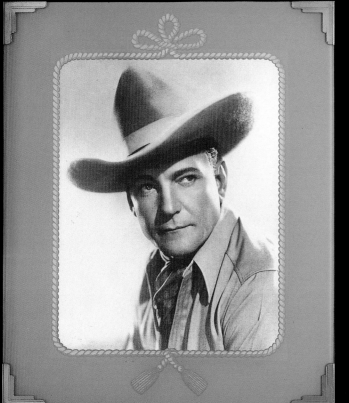

Left:
Circa 1938. Silk-screened in turquoise, ivory, and metallic silver on ⅛"-thick glass. Mounted to an easel back by chrome-plated steel corner clips.
Size: 11 x 13".
Window: 7⁵/₁₆ X 9⁵/₁₆".
Photo: Buck Jones.

Opposite:
Circa 1940. Silk-screened in ivory, maroon, and metallic gold on ⅛"-thick glass. Mounted to an easel back by chrome-plated steel corner clips. Size: 11 x 13".
Window: 7¼ X 9³/₁₆".
Photo: Marlene Dietrich.

Below:
Circa 1938. Silk-screened in
black, ivory, and metallic gold
on ⅛"-thick glass. Mounted to
an easel back by chrome-plated
steel corner clips. Size: 11 x 13".
Window: 7¼ x 9¼".
Photo: Marjorie Weaver.

Below:
Circa 1937. Silk-screened in
metallic gold, accented with silver
mirroring, on ¼"-thick glass with
a hand-tooled scalloped edge.
Glued to an easel back.
Size: 11 x 13".
Window: 7³⁄₁₆ x 9³⁄₁₆".
Photo: Louise Hovick
(Gypsy Rose Lee).

Opposite:
Circa 1936. Silk-screened in
black, green and metallic gold,
accented with silver mirroring on
⅛"-thick glass. Mounted to an
easel back by nickel-plated steel
rosettes. Size: 10 x 12".
Window: 6¹³⁄₁₆ x 8¹³⁄₁₆".
Photo: Rosemary Lane.

Left:
Circa 1935. Hand-engraved
¼"-thick glass. Mounted to a
velvet-covered easel back lined
on one side with modernist-
patterned paper by chrome-plated
steel rosettes with amber-colored
acrylic bolts. Size: 12 x 14".
Window: 7½ x 9½".
Photo: Jean Parker.

Left:
Circa 1936. Clear ⅛"-thick glass,
decorated with a hand-painted
floral design in pink, rose, yellow,
gold, and green. Mounted to an
easel back by nickel-plated steel
rosettes. Size: 9¹⁵⁄₁₆ X 12".
Window: 7 x 9".
Photo: Eleanor Powell.

Opposite:
Circa 1946. Sandblasted leaf
design on ¼"-thick, hand-beveled
glass. Mounted to an easel back
by nickel-plated steel rosettes.
Size:14 x 17".
Window: 7½ x 9½".
Photo: Rita Hayworth.

Above:
Circa 1934. Silk-screened in black, cream, and metallic silver on ⅛"-thick glass. Mounted to an easel back by chrome-plated steel corner clips. Size: 7 x 9". Window: 4³⁄₁₆ x 3⅞". Photo: Eddie "Rochester" Anderson.

Above:
Circa 1933. Silk-screened in black, ivory, and cream on ⅛"-thick glass. Mounted to an easel back by nickel-plated steel corner clips. Size: 5 x 6". Window: 2⅞ x 3⅞". Photo: Lois Moran.

metric

Geometric patterns in the Art Deco style crossed the Atlantic with Americans influenced by the decorative objects on display at the 1925 Paris decorative arts exposition. The patterns were expressive of a new modernism and were applied to a range of objects, including glass photo frames.

Above:
Circa 1929. Silk-screened in black, ivory, and metallic gold on ⅛"-thick glass. Mounted to an easel back by nickel-plated brass corner clips. Size: 7 x 9". Window: 6³⁄₁₆ X 4¼". Photo: Gertrude Olmsted.

Virginia
Bruce

M.G.M. PICTURES

Page 54:
Circa 1931. Silk-screened in ivory, black, and sienna, accented with silver mirroring, on 1/8"-thick glass. Held on an easel back by a framing of 3/16"-wide textured brass. Size: 10 x 12". Window: 7 5/16 X 9 5/16". Photo: Bebe Daniels.

Page 55:
Circa 1933. Silk-screened in ivory, black, and metallic gold on 1/8"-thick glass. Glued to an easel back. Size: 10 x 12". Window: 7 x 9 1/8". Photo: Virginia Bruce.

Above:
Circa 1933. Silk-screened in black on 1/8"-thick glass, backed by a metallic silver paper mat. Held on an easel back by a framing of 5/16"-wide chrome-plated steel. Size: 10 1/2 x 12 1/2". Window: 6 15/16 X 8 15/16". Photo: Anna May Wong.

Above:
Circa 1931. Silk-screened in black on 1/8"-thick glass, backed by a metallic silver paper mat. Held on an easel back by a framing of 5/16"-wide chrome-plated steel. Size: 5 x 6 1/2". Window: 2 7/8 x 3 7/8". Photo: Sally Blane.

Left:
Circa 1928. Silk-screened in black on ⅛"-thick glass, backed by a textured metallic silver paper mat. Held on an easel back by a framing of ⁵⁄₁₆"-wide chrome-plated steel. Size: 8½ X 10½". Window: 4³⁄₁₆ X 6³⁄₁₆".
Photo: Richard Arlen.

With Best Wishes
Richard Arlen

Paramount Studios.

Best wishes
Mary Brian

Paramount
Studios

Sincerely
Colleen Moore

Left:
Circa 1928. Silk-screened in black, accented with silver mirroring and hand-engraved frosted lines, on ⅛"-thick glass. Mounted to an easel back by nickel-plated brass corner clips.
Size: 7½ x 9½".
Window: 6¹⁵/₁₆ x 4¹⁵/₁₆".
Photo: Corinne Griffith.

Left:
Circa 1933. Silk-screened in ivory and black, accented with silver mirroring, on ⅛"-thick glass. Mounted to an easel back by nickel-plated steel rosettes.
Size: 10 x 12".
Window: 6/₁₆ x 8⁷/₁₆".
Photo: Mae West.

Opposite:
Circa 1929. Silk-screened in beige, black, and metallic gold on ⅛"-thick glass. Mounted to an easel back by brass-plated steel corner clips. Size: 4½ x 5½".
Window: 3⁷/₁₆ x 2⁷/₁₆".
Photo: Ronald Colman.

Below:
Circa 1933. Silk-screened in
ultramarine blue and black,
accented with silver mirroring,
on ⅛"-thick glass. Mounted to
an easel back with embossed
steel bands. Size: 4½ X 6".
Window: 2¾ X 3⅝".
Photo: Joan Bennett.

Opposite:
Circa 1930. Silk-screened in
turquoise, ivory, and metallic
silver on ⅛"-thick glass. Mounted
to an easel back by chrome-
plated steel corner clips.
Size: 10 x 12".
Window: 6¹⁵/₁₆ X 8⅜".
Photo: Jean Harlow.

Below:
Circa 1928. Silk-screened in black, white, and ivory on ⅛"-thick glass. Mounted to an easel back by nickel-plated steel corner clips. Size: 8 x 10".
Window: 4³⁄₁₆ x 6¼".
Photo: Charles "Buddy" Rogers.

Below:
Circa 1933. Silk-screened in black, ivory, and metallic gold on ⅛"-thick glass. Mounted to an easel back by chrome-plated steel corner clips. Size: 6 x 8".
Window: 3 x 4⁷⁄₁₆".
Photo: Franchot Tone.

Opposite:
Circa 1927. Silk-screened in black, gold, and ivory on ⅛"-thick glass. Held on an easel back by a framing of ribbed brass, accented with black lacquer. Size: 7½ x 9".
Window: 4½ x 6½".
Photo: Dolores Costello.

Dolores Costello

Right:
Circa 1929. Silk-screened in metallic gold and forest green, accented with silver mirroring, on ⅛"-thick glass. Mounted to an easel back by nickel-plated steel rosettes. Size: 10 x 12". Window: 6⅝ x 8¾".
Photo: Evelyn Brent.

Above:
Circa 1930. Silk-screened in black and red, accented with silver mirroring, on ⅛"-thick glass. Mounted to an easel back by nickel-plated steel bands. Size: 4 x 5". Window: 2½ x 3½".
Photo: Dorothy Lee.

Right:
Circa 1934. Silk-screened in deep coral, accented with silver mirroring, on ⅛"-thick glass. Mounted to an easel back by chrome-plated steel bands. Size: 2¾ x 3½".
Window: 1⅜ x 1¾".
Photo: Robert Taylor.

Right:
Circa 1932. Silk-screened in
ivory, black and metallic silver on
⅛"-thick glass Mounted to an
easel back by chrome-plated steel
corner clips. Size: 8 x 10".
Window: 6³⁄₁₆ x 8¼".
Photo: Madge Evans.

Overleaf left:
Circa 1932. Silk-screened in
black and metallic silver on
⅛"-thick glass. Glued to an
easel back. Size: 10 x 12".
Window: 7³⁄₈ x 9¼".
Photo: Merle Oberon.

Overleaf right:
Circa 1929. Silk-screened in
black, taupe, and metallic gold
on ⅛"-thick glass. Mounted to
an easel back by chrome-plated
brass corner clips. Size: 7 x 9".
Window: 3³⁄₈ x 5½".
Photo: Nancy Carroll.

Fondest Wishes
Nancy Carroll

Right:
Circa 1929. Silk-screened in lilac and black, accented with silver mirroring, on ⅛"-thick glass. Held on an easel back by a framing of ¼"-wide nickel-plated brass. Size: 10 x 12½". Window: 6⅞ x 8⅞". Photo: Myrna Loy.

Right:
Circa 1932. Silk-screened in black and blue-gray, accented with silver mirroring, on ⅛"-thick glass. Mounted to an easel back by nickel-plated steel rosettes. Size: 10 x 12". Window: 6¾ x 8¾". Photo: Kay Francis.

Opposite:
Circa 1934. Silk-screened in cream and metallic gold, accented with silver mirroring, on ⅛"-thick glass. Mounted to an easel back by chrome-plated steel corner clips. Size: 10 x 12". Window: 7 x 9". Photo: Miriam Hopkins.

Miriam Hokk

The designs applied to many frames of the 1930s and 1940s reflect the popular, rather urbane taste for simplicity and clean, line-based decoration. Frames adorned with such motifs as stepped skyscraper and other architectural forms, speed lines, and nautical elements, and often embellished with sections of colored mirror, are categorized under Moderne.

Opposite:
Circa 1935. Silk-screened in sienna and ivory, accented with silver mirroring, on $1/8$"-thick glass. Mounted to an easel back by chrome-plated steel corner clips. Size: 10 x 12".
Window: $6^{15}/_{16}$ X $8^{3}/_{4}$".
Photo: Mary Carlisle.

M
O
D
E
R
N
E

Mary Carlisle
in Paramount Pictures

Below:
Circa 1938. ⅝"-wide aluminum framing, trimmed with bronze-tinted aluminum. Manufactured by Kensington. Size: 8¼ x 10¼". Window: 7 x 9". Photo: Marion Davies.

Above:
Circa 1944. Clear ¼"-thick glass with hand-engraved lines outlining window area, surrounded by strips of hand-beveled ¼"-thick mirror, attached with silver-plated brass corner brackets. Mounted to an easel back by rosette screws with clear blown-glass heads. Size: 12 x 14". Window area: 7¾ x 9¾". Photo: Ann Sheridan.

Dorothy Lamour

Below:
Circa 1931. Silk-screened in maroon, taupe, and metallic gold on 1/8"-thick glass. Held on an easel back by a framing of 3/8"-wide brass. Size: 8 x 10". Window: 4¾ x 6¾". Photo: Barbara Stanwyck.

Below:
Circa 1939. Silk-screened in teal, gray, and metallic gold on 1/8"-thick glass. Mounted to an easel back by solid brass corner clips. Size: 5 x 7". Window: 2¾ x 3¾". Photo: Lynda Darnell.

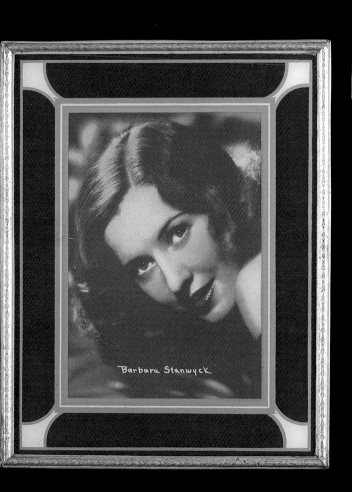

Above:
Circa 1935. ¾"-wide bronze
framing trimmed with silver.
Manufactured by Silvercrest
Bronze. Size: 9¼ x 11¼".
Window: 7¹¹/₁₆ x 9¹¹/₁₆".
Photo: Bette Davis.

Above:
Circa 1935. ⅝"-wide bronze
framing, accented with black
silk-screened ⅛"-thick glass.
Manufactured by Romart.
Size: 8¹⁵/₁₆ x 11".
Window: 7½ x 9½".
Photo: Joan Crawford.

Opposite:
Circa 1937. Silk-screened in black. ivory, and metallic olive on 1/8"-thick glass. Mounted to an easel back by nickel-plated steel corner clips. Size: 5 x 7".
Window: 4¹³/₁₆ x 2¹³/₁₆".
Photo: George Sanders.

Above:
Circa 1941. Silk-screened in maroon, ivory, and metallic gold on 1/8"-thick glass. Mounted to an easel back by chrome-plated steel corner clips. Size: 7 x 9".
Window: 4¼ x 6¼".
Photo: Greer Garson.

Above:
Circa 1934. Silk-screened in ivory, mint green, and metallic gold on 1/8"-thick glass. Mounted to an easel back by chrome-plated steel corner clips.
Size 6 x 8". Window: 3 x 4¾".
Photo: Ruby Keeler.

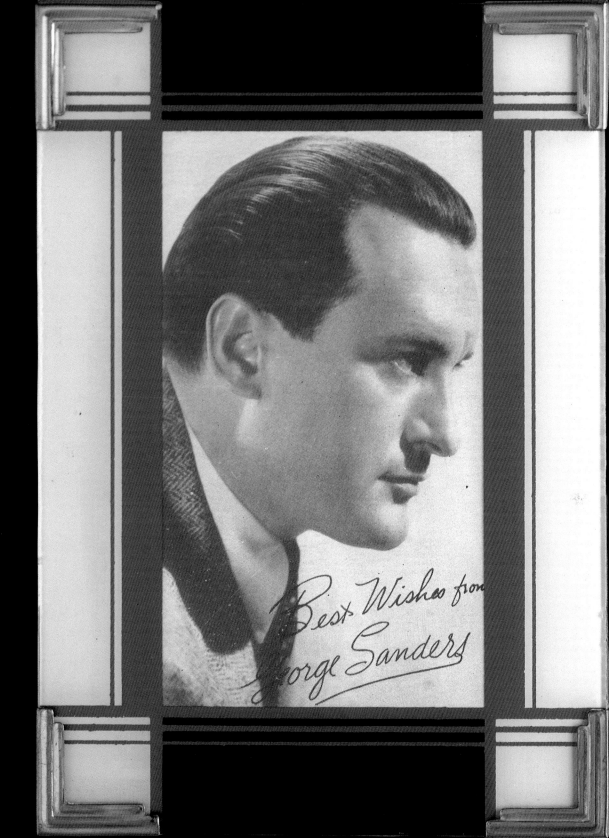

Best Wishes from George Sanders

George Raft

Opposite:
Circa 1934. Silk-screened in
black and metallic gold on
⅛"-thick glass. Mounted to an
easel back by metallic gold-
painted steel corner clips.
Size: 10 x 12".
Window: 6⅝ x 8⅝".
Photo: George Raft.

Overleaf left:
Circa 1935. Silk-screened in
metallic gold on ⅛"-thick glass.
Mounted to an easel back by
metallic gold-painted steel
rosettes. Size: 11 x 13".
Window: 7½ x 9⁹⁄₁₆".
Photo: Sylvia Sidney.

Overleaf right:
Circa 1941. Hand-beveled,
hand-engraved, and mirrored
¼"-thick glass. Mounted to a
velvet-covered easel back by
nickel-plated screws.
Size: 11¹⁵⁄₁₆ x 13⅞".
Window: 7½ x 9¼".
Photo: Hedy LaMarr.

Above:
Circa 1935. Silk-screened in
black and metallic gold on
⅛"-thick glass. Held on an easel
back by a framing of ¼"-wide
brass. Size: 10 x 18".
Window: 7¼ x 9¼".
Photo: Robert Young.

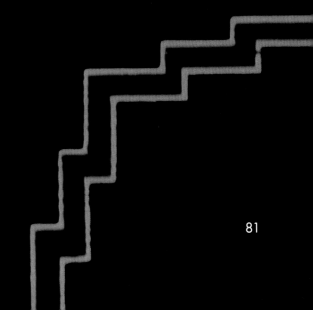

Sylvia Sidney
WALTER WANGER FILMS

PRINTED IN U. S. A.

Above:
Circa 1934. Silk-screened in
metallic silver, black, and cream
on ⅛"-thick glass. Mounted to an
easel back by chrome-plated steel
corner clips. Size: 11 x 13".
Window: 7¹¹⁄₁₆ x 9¹¹⁄₁₆".
Photo: Ann Harding.

Below:
Circa 1946. 1½"-wide brass framing plated in 24-karat gold. Size: 9¹⁵/₁₆ x 11³/₈".
Window: 6¹⁵/₁₆ x 9".
Photo: Alexis Smith.

Below:
Circa 1942. ⁵/₈"-wide chrome-plated brass framing. Size: 6⁷/₈ x 8⁷/₈".
Window: 5⁹/₁₆ x 7⁵/₈".
Photo: Alice Faye.

Opposite:
Circa 1934. Silk-screened in black with clear areas on ⅛"-thick glass, backed by a metallic silver paper mat. Held on an easel back by a framing of ³/₈"-wide chrome-plated steel.
Size: 10 x 12⅛".
Window: 7 x 8¹⁵/₁₆".
Photo: Grace Moore.

86

Above:
Circa 1931. Silk-screened in ivory
and black, accented with silver
mirroring, on ⅛"-thick glass.
Mounted to an easel back by
nickel-plated steel corner clips.
Size: 10 x 12".
Window: 6⅜ x 8¾".
Photo: Marion Davies.

Above:
Circa 1935. Silk-screened in ivory
and black, accented with silver
mirroring, on ⅛"-thick glass.
Mounted to an easel back by
nickel-plated steel rosettes.
Size: 10 x 12". Arched
window: 6⅝ x 8⅝".
Photo: Ethel Merman.

Below:
Circa 1938. Silk-screened in
black, accented with silver
mirroring, on ⅛"-thick glass.
Glued to an easel back.
Size: 10 x 12".
Window: 6⅞ x 8¾".
Photo: James Cagney.

Below:
Circa 1935. Silk-screened in
black and metallic silver on
⅛"-thick glass. Held on an easel
back by a framing of ¼"-wide
nickel-plated steel. Size: 10 x 12".
Window: 6⁵⁄₁₆ x 9⅞".
Photo: Robert Montgomery.

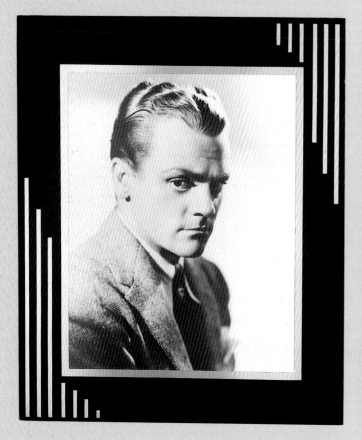

Opposite:
Circa 1938. Silk-screened in
black, accented with silver
mirroring, on ⅛"-thick glass.
Mounted to an easel back by
nickel-plated steel rosettes.
Size: 9⅞ x 11¹⁵⁄₁₆".
Oval window: 7⅛ x 9⅛".
Photo: Charles Boyer.

Charles Boyer
IN
METRO GOLDWYN-MAYER PICTURES

Right:
Circa 1935. Silk-screened in
ivory, black, and metallic gold on
1/8"-thick glass. Mounted to an
easel back by nickel-plated steel
rosettes. Size: 11 x 13".
Window: 6¹¹/₁₆ x 8¹¹/₁₆".
Photo: Clark Gable.

Right:
Circa 1934. Silk-screened in ivory
and black, with hand-engraved
lines painted in metallic gold, on
1/8"-thick glass. Mounted to an
easel back by nickel-plated steel
rosettes. Size: 9¹⁵/₁₆ x 11¹⁵/₁₆".
Window: 6³/₄ x 8³/₄".
Photo: John Boles.

Opposite:
Circa 1934. Silk-screened in ivory
and black with clear areas on
1/8"-thick glass, backed by a silver
foil mat. Held on an easel back
with a framing of 5/₁₆"-wide
chrome-plated steel.
Size: 10 x 12".
Window: 6⁷/₈ x 8⁷/₈".
Photo: Carole Lombard.

Below:
Circa 1934. Silk-screened in metallic silver, ivory, and black on ⅛"-thick glass. Held on an easel back by a framing of ⅜"-wide chrome-plated steel.
Size: 10 x 12".
Window: 6⅞ x 8⅞".
Photo: Fred Astaire.

Below:
Circa 1934. Silk-screened in metallic silver, ivory, and black on ⅛"-thick glass. Held on an easel back by a framing of ⅜"-wide chrome-plated steel.
Size: 10 x 12".
Window: 6⅞ x 8⅞".
Photo: Ginger Rogers.

Opposite:
Circa 1935. Silk-screened in metallic silver, black, and cream on ⅛"-thick glass. Held on an easel back by a framing of 5/16"-wide chrome-plated steel.
Size: 10 1/16 x 12".
Window: 6 15/16 x 8 13/16".
Photo: Gary Cooper.

Below:
Circa 1934. Silk-screened in ivory, accented with silver mirroring, on ⅛"-thick glass. Glued to an easel back.
Size: 10 x 12".
Window: 6¹³⁄₁₆ X 9⁹⁄₁₆".
Photo: Norma Shearer.

Below:
Circa 1935. Silk-screened in ivory and metallic silver, accented with silver mirroring, on ⅛"-thick glass. Mounted to an easel back by nickel-plated steel rosettes.
Size: 10 x 12".
Window: 7¹⁄₁₆ X 9⁹⁄₁₆".
Photo: Katharine Hepburn.

Opposite:
Circa 1936. Peach-tinted, mirrored, ¼"-thick, hand-engraved, and hand-beveled glass. Glued to an easel back.
Size: 10 x 12".
Window: 7½ X 9½".
Photo: Gloria Stuart.

Gloria Stuart
20th Century Fox Pictures

Printed in U. S. A.

Below:
Circa 1939. Silk-screened in black, ivory, and metallic gold on 1/8"-thick glass. Mounted to an easel back by chrome-plated steel corner clips. Size: 7 x 9". Window: 6³/₁₆ x 4³/₁₆". Photo: Shirley Temple.

Opposite:
Circa 1931. Silk-screened in black, ivory, and metallic gold on 1/8"-thick glass. Mounted to an easel back by chrome-plated brass corner clips. Size: 7 x 9". Window: 3⁹/₁₆ x 5¹/₂". Photo: Betty Compson.

Sincerely yours,
Betty Compson.

Left:
Circa 1939. Silk-screened in maroon, ivory, and metallic gold on ⅛"-thick glass. Mounted to an easel back by brass-plated steel corner clips. Size: 10 x 12". Window: 6³⁄₈ x 8⁷⁄₁₆". Photo: Jeanette MacDonald.

Left:
Circa 1935. Silk-screened in ivory, green, and metallic gold on ⅛"-thick glass. Mounted to an easel back by chrome-plated steel corner clips. Size: 11 x 13". Window: 7¼ x 9¼". Photo: Fredric March.

Above:
Circa 1938. Silk-screened in
violet, accented with silver
mirroring, on ⅛"-thick glass.
Held on an easel back by a
framing of ¼"-wide nickel-
plated steel. Size: 10⅛ x 12⅛".
Window: 6⅞ x 8⅞".
Photo: Rosalind Russell.

Below:
Circa 1942. Silk-screened in
black, ivory, and metallic gold on
1/8"-thick glass. Mounted to an
easel back by polished steel
corner clips. Size: 3 1/2 x 4 7/16".
Window: 1 13/16 x 2 13/16".
Photo: Robert Taylor.

Below:
Circa 1942. Silk-screened in
ivory, black, and metallic gold on
1/8"-thick glass. Mounted to an
easel back by polished steel
corner clips. Size: 3 1/2 x 4 7/16".
Window: 1 13/16 x 2 13/16".
Photo: Veronica Lake.

Opposite:
Circa 1935. Silk-screened in
black and silver on 1/8"-thick
glass. Held on an easel back by a
framing of 3/8"-wide chrome-
plated steel. Size: 10 x 12 1/8".
Window: 7 3/16 x 9 1/8".
Photo: Spencer Tracy.

Opposite:
Circa 1935. Silk-screened in ivory, black, and metallic gold on ⅛"-thick glass. Mounted to an easel back by brass corner clips. Size: 5 x 7".
Window: 2¹³/₁₆ x 4¹³/₁₆".
Photo: Bruce Cabot.

Above:
Circa 1942. Silk-screened in crystallized metallic gold, accented with silver mirroring, on ⅛"-thick glass. Mounted to an easel back by nickel-plated steel rosettes. Size: 9¼ x 12".
Window: 6¾ x 8¾".
Photo: Billie Burke.

Above:
Circa 1942. Silk-screened in beige, black, and metallic gold on ⅛"-thick glass. Held on an easel back by a framing of ⅜"-wide brass. Size: 10¹/₁₆ x 12¹/₁₆".
Window: 7¼ x 9¼".
Photo: Lucille Ball.

Cordially
Bruce Cabot

105

Opposite:
Circa 1937. Silk-screened in black, ivory, and metallic silver on ⅛"-thick glass. Mounted to an easel back by chrome-plated steel corner clips. Size: 8 x 10". Window: 4¹³/₁₆ x 6¹³/₁₆".
Photo: Loretta Young.

Above:
Circa 1936. Silk-screened in black and ivory, accented with silver mirroring, on ⅛"-thick glass. Mounted to an easel back by nickel-plated steel rosettes. Size: 10 x 12". Circular window: 7⅛" diameter.
Photo: Irene Dunne.

Below:
Circa 1930. Silk-screened in black and turquoise with clear areas on ⅛"-thick glass, backed by a textured silver foil mat. Mounted to an easel back by nickel-plated steel corner clips. Size: 5¹⁵/₁₆ x 7¹⁵/₁₆". Window: 2¾ x 3¾". Photo: Jean Arthur.

Below:
Circa 1942. ¾"-wide nickel-plated brass framing trimmed with light blue and dark blue enamel. Size: 7¹⁵/₁₆ x 10½". Window: 6½ x 9". Photo: Ginger Rogers.

Opposite:
Circa 1936. Silk-screened in white on ⅛"-thick cobalt-blue tinted glass. Mounted to an easel back by nickel-plated steel rosettes. Size: 7½ x 9½". Window: 4⅞ x 6⅞". Photo: Fay Wray.

Above:
Circa 1934. Silk-screened in ivory, black, and brown on 1/8"-thick glass. Held on an easel back by a framing of 1/4"-wide chrome-plated steel.
Size: 10 1/16 x 12 1/16".
Window: 7 1/4 x 9 1/4".
Photo: Shirley Temple.

Opposite:
Circa 1942. Silk-screened in ivory, black, and metallic gold on ⅛"-thick glass. Mounted to an easel back by chrome-plated steel corner clips. Size: 10 x 12". Window: 7¼ x 9¼".
Photo: Van Johnson.

Above:
Circa 1937. 1⅛"-wide strips of mirrored, ⅛"-thick blue cobalt glass surrounding ⅛"-thick clear glass. Mounted to an easel back by chrome-plated steel corner clips. Size: 10 x 12". Window: 7¾ x 9¾".
Photo: Carole Lombard.

Strean

Above:
Circa 1936. Silk-screened in black and cream on ⅛"-thick glass. Held on an easel back by a framing of ⁵/₁₆"-wide chrome-plated steel. Size: 5 x 7". Window: 2¹⁵/₁₆ x 4¹⁵/₁₆". Photo: Jon Hall.

ined

Curved lines, circles, and other simple forms seemingly created to imitate aerodynamic speed characterize Streamlined frame designs. In many cases, the corners of the window area are rounded, though the rectangular shape of the frame remains intact.

Above:
Circa 1936. Silk-screened in black, accented with silver mirroring, on ⅛"-thick glass. Mounted to an easel back by chrome-plated steel rosettes. Size: 10 x 12". Arched window: 6¾ x 8¹¹/₁₆". Photo: Gene Raymond.

Above:
Circa 1939. Silk-screened in
black, metallic gold, and pink on
⅛"-thick glass. Mounted to an
easel back by chrome-plated
brass corner clips.
Size: 7 x 10". Arched
window: 4½ x 6½".
Photo: Mickey Rooney.

Above:
Circa 1939. Silk-screened in
beige, metallic gold, and cobalt
blue on ⅛"-thick glass. Mounted
to an easel back by chrome-
plated brass corner clips.
Size: 7 x 10". Arched
window: 4½ x 6½".
Photo: Judy Garland.

Below:
Circa 1936. Silk-screened in ivory, black, and metallic gold on ⅛"-thick glass. Mounted to an easel back by chrome-plated steel corner clips. Size: 8 x 9¹⁵/₁₆".
Window: 4⁷/₁₆ x 6½".
Photo: Lew Ayres.

Below:
Circa 1936. Silk-screened in black, ivory, and metallic gold on ⅛"-thick glass. Mounted to an easel back by chrome-plated steel corner clips. Size: 8 x 9¹⁵/₁₆".
Window: 4⁷/₁₆ x 6½".
Photo: Madeleine Carroll.

Below:
Circa 1936. Silk-screened in
ivory, black, and metallic gold
on ⅛"-thick glass. Mounted to
an easel back by chrome-plated
steel corner clips. Size: 8 x 9¹⁵/₁₆".
Window: 4⁷/₁₆ x 6½".
Photo: Lew Ayres.

Below:
Circa 1936. Silk-screened in
black, ivory, and metallic gold
on ⅛"-thick glass. Mounted to
an easel back by chrome-plated
steel corner clips. Size: 8 x 9¹⁵/₁₆".
Window: 4⁷/₁₆ x 6½".
Photo: Madeleine Carroll.

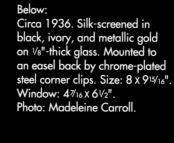

Opposite:
Circa 1942. Silk-screened in
ivory, metallic gold, and black
on ⅛"-thick glass. Mounted to
an easel back with polished steel
corner clips. Size: 4½ x 3½".
Window: 1¹³/₁₆ x 2¹³/₁₆".
Photo: Susanna Foster.

Right:
Circa 1939. Silk-screened in black, ivory, and metallic gold on ⅛"-thick glass. Mounted to an easel back by chrome-plated steel corner clips. Size: 7 x 9". Undulating window: 4³⁄₁₆ x 6³⁄₁₆".
Photo: Myrna Loy.

Above:
Circa 1943. Silk-screened in maroon, metallic gold, and ivory on ⅛"-thick glass. Mounted to an easel back by brass-plated steel corner clips. Size: 8 x 10". Window: 4½ x 6½".
Photo: Robert Taylor.

Right:
Circa 1937. Silk-screened in black and ivory, accented with silver mirroring, on ⅛"-thick glass. Held on an easel back by a framing of ¼"-wide brass. Size: 10⅛ x 12⅛". Window: 6⅞ x 8⅞".
Photo: Deanna Durbin.

Overleaf left:
Circa 1937. Silk-screened in
blue and orchid, accented with
silver mirroring, on ¼"-thick
glass with a hand-tooled
scalloped edge. Mounted to
an easel back by nickel-plated
steel rosettes. Size: 11 x 13".
Window: 7³/₁₆ x 9¼".
Photo: Myrna Loy.

Overleaf right:
Circa 1937. Silk-screened in
pale olive and green, accented
with silver mirroring, on ¼"-thick
glass with a hand-tooled
scalloped edge. Mounted to an
easel back by nickel-plated steel
rosettes. Size: 11 x 13".
Window: 7³/₁₆ x 9³/₁₆".
Photo: Madeleine Carroll.

Above:
Circa 1941. Silk-screened in
ivory, metallic gold, and black
on ⅛"-thick glass. Mounted to
an easel back by chrome-plated
steel corner clips. Size: 10 x 12".
Window: 7³/₁₆ x 9³/₁₆".
Photo: Humphrey Bogart.

Opposite, top left:
Circa 1940. Silk-screened in
maroon and ivory, accented with
silver mirroring, on ¼"-thick glass
with a hand-tooled scalloped
edge. Mounted to an easel back
by nickel-plated steel rosettes.
Size: 11 x 13".
Window: 7³/₁₆ X 9³/₁₆".
Photo: Hedy LaMarr.

Opposite, top right:
Circa 1940. Silk-screened in ivory
and maroon, accented with silver
mirroring, on ¼"-thick glass with a
hand-tooled scalloped edge.
Mounted to an easel back by
nickel-plated steel rosettes.
Size: 11 x 13".
Window: 7³/₁₆ X 9³/₁₆".
Photo: Hedy LaMarr.

Above:
Circa 1940. Silk-screened in
black and metallic gold, accented
with silver mirroring, on ¼"-thick
glass with a hand-tooled
scalloped edge. Mounted to an
easel back by nickel-plated steel
rosettes. Size: 11 x 13".
Window: 6³/₄ x 8¹¹/₁₆".
Photo: Hedy LaMarr.

Opposite, bottom left:
Circa 1940. Silk-screened in pale
celery and maroon, accented with
silver mirroring, on ¼"-thick glass
with a hand-tooled scalloped
edge. Mounted to an easel back
by nickel-plated steel rosettes.
Size: 11 x 13".
Window: 7³/₁₆ X 9³/₁₆".
Photo: Hedy LaMarr.

Opposite, bottom right:
Circa 1940. Silk-screened in sky
blue and ivory, accented with
silver mirroring, on ¼"-thick glass
with a hand-tooled scalloped
edge. Mounted to an easel back
by nickel-plated steel rosettes.
Size: 11 x 13".
Window: 7³/₁₆ X 9³/₁₆".
Photo: Hedy LaMarr.

Left:
Circa 1940. Silk-screened in sand and cerulean blue on ¼"-thick glass. Mounted to an easel back by nickel-plated steel rosettes.
Size: 11 x 13".
Window: 7⅛ x 9⅛".
Photo: Bette Davis.

Left:
Circa 1938. Silk-screened in ivory and sienna, accented with silver mirroring, on ⅛"-thick glass. Held on an easel back with a framing of 3/16"- wide chrome-plated steel.
Size: 10 x 12".
Window: 6⅞ x 8¹³/₁₆".
Photo: Loretta Young.

Opposite:
Circa 1938. Silk-screened in gray and aqua, accented with gold mirroring, on ¼"-thick glass with a hand-tooled scalloped edge. Mounted to an easel back by chrome-plated steel rosettes.
Size: 10 x 12". Window: 7 x 9".
Photo: Ann Sothern.

MG73520

Above:
Circa 1938. Silk-screened in
beige, black, and metallic silver
on 1/8"-thick glass. Mounted to an
easel back by chrome-plated steel
corner clips. Size: 11 x 13".
Window: 7 3/4 x 9 3/4".
Photo: Don Ameche.

Above:
Circa 1937. Silk-screened in
ivory, chocolate, and metallic
gold on 1/8"-thick glass. Held
on an easel back by a framing
of 3/16"-wide brass-plated steel
with brushed-brass striping.
Size: 10 1/16 x 12 1/16".
Window: 6 11/16 x 8 11/16".
Photo: Alice Faye.

Overleaf left:
Circa 1939. Silk-screened
in ivory, accented with silver
mirroring, on 1/8"-thick glass.
Glued to an easel back.
Size: 10 x 12". Arched
window: 7 1/8 x 9 1/2".
Photo: Mary Martin.

Overleaf right:
Circa 1941. Silk-screened in
cream, accented with silver
mirroring, on 1/8"-thick glass.
Mounted to an easel back by
nickel-plated steel rosettes.
Size: 10 x 12".
Window: 7 1/8 x 9 1/16".
Photo: Carmen Miranda.

Above:
Circa 1938. Silk-screened in
black, cream, and metallic gold
on 1/8"-thick glass. Glued to an
easel back. Size: 5 1/2 x 7".
Window: 2 3/4 x 3 3/4".
Photo: Cary Grant.

Above:
Circa 1938. Silk-screened in
coral, cream, and metallic gold
on 1/8"-thick glass. Glued to an
easel back. Size: 5 1/2 x 7".
Window: 2 3/4 x 3 3/4".
Photo: Joel McCrea.

Mary Martin

Below:
Circa 1939. Silk-screened in ivory, black, and metallic gold on ⅛"-thick glass. Mounted to an easel back by polished steel corner clips. Size: 5½ x 7½". Window: 3⅛ x 5⅛". Photo: Bob Hope.

Cordially, Bob Hope

100% AMERICAN

CAMP ROBINSON

PATRIOTIC

During the World War II years, American frame designers and manufacturers produced patriotic-themed products. The red, white, and blue palette figures prominently in the designs of the frames, often embellished with silver or gold mirroring effects. Patriotic frames were usually sold containing a photograph of a uniformed movie star, a favorite pin-up girl, or even a famous general.

Opposite:
Circa 1943. Silk-screened in red, white, and blue, accented with silver mirroring, on 1/8"-thick glass. Mounted to an easel back with chrome-plated steel bands.
Size: 5¹⁵/₁₆ X 4⁵/₁₆".
Window: 2³/₄ X 3³/₄".
Photo: Unidentified enlisted man (Photo most likely taken at the USO Service Club, Camp Robinson, North Little Rock, Arkansas).

Above:
Circa 1942. 1/2"-wide steel framing, with a simulated walnut finish, and 1/8"-thick clear glass, backed with a paper mat printed in a red, white, and blue design.
Size: 5⁷/₁₆ X 7⁷/₁₆".
Mat window: 3³/₈ X 5⁵/₁₆".
Photo: Wayne Morris.

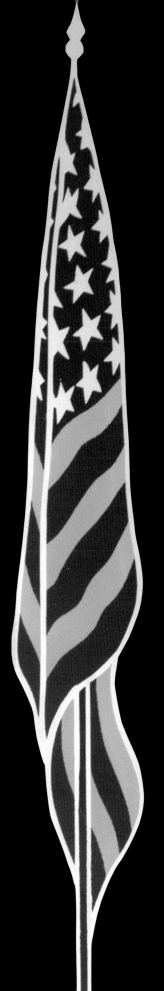

Below:
Circa 1943. Silk-screened in red, white, and blue, accented with silver mirroring, on 1/8"-thick glass. Held on an easel back by a framing of 1/4"-wide natural pine. Size: 10^{11}/$_{16}$ X 12^{11}/$_{16}$".
Window: 6^9/$_{16}$ X 9^9/$_{16}$".
Photo: June Preisser.

Opposite:
Circa 1943. Silk-screened in red, white, and blue on 1/8"-thick glass. Held on an easel back by a framing of ivory lacquered wood. Size: 10^5/$_8$ X 12^{11}/$_{16}$".
Window: 6^{15}/$_{16}$ X 8^{15}/$_{16}$".
Photo: Judy Garland.

Page 138:
Circa 1943. Silk-screened in red, white, blue, and metallic silver on 1/8"-thick glass. Mounted to an easl back by nickel-plated steel rosettes and chrome-plated steel corner clips. Size: 8 x 10".
Window: 6^{15}/$_{16}$ X 8^{15}/$_{16}$".
Photo: Lana Turner.

Page 139:
Circa 1945. Silk-screened in red, white, and blue, accented with silver mirroring, on 1/8"-thick glass. Mounted to an easel back by nickel-plated steel rosettes.
Size: 9^7/$_8$ x 12".
Window: 6^{13}/$_{16}$ X 8^7/$_8$".
Photo: Betty Hutton.

Sincerely
Judy Garland

BETTY HUTTON
in Paramount Pictures

P2820-N398

Below:
Circa 1942. "Victory Metal Photo Frame." $1/8$"-thick clear glass backed by a removable paper mat printed in a red, white, and blue design. Held on an easel back by a framing of embossed nickel-plated steel. Manufactured by Art Publishing Company. Size: 8 x 10".
Mat window: 5 x 7".
Photo: James Stewart.

Below:
Circa 1943. Silk-screened in red, white, and blue on $1/8$"-thick glass. Mounted to an easel back by chrome-plated steel corner clips. Size: 8 x 10".
Window: $6^{1}/_8$ x $4^{3}/_{16}$".
Photo: John Payne.

Opposite:
Circa 1942. Silk-screened in red, white, blue, and metallic gold on $1/8$"-thick glass. Mounted to an easel back by solid brass corner clips. Size: 7 x 9".
Window: $4^{7}/_{16}$ x $6^{7}/_{16}$".
Photo: Preston Foster.

In the
Service of his Country

Below:
Circa 1942. Silk-screened in red, white, and blue, accented with silver mirroring, on $1/8$"-thick glass. Mounted to an easel back by chrome-plated steel corner clips. Size: 8 x 9".
Window: $4^{3}/_{16}$ X $3^{11}/_{16}$".
Photo: Tyrone Power.

FOR GOD AND COUNTRY

Opposite:
Circa 1943. Silk-screened in red, white, and blue, accented with silver mirroring, on $1/8$"-thick glass. Held on an easel back by a framing of $1/4$"-wide metallic gold-painted and cream lacquered pine.
Size: $10^{11}/_{16}$ X $12^{11}/_{16}$".
Window: $6^{11}/_{16}$ X $9^{1}/_{16}$".
Photo: Robert Taylor.

ROBERT TAYLOR · Metro Goldwyn Mayer

Left:
Circa 1936. "Remember Me" greeting frame. Heart-shaped window and puppy design silk-screened in red, cream, and metallic silver on ⅛"-thick glass. Mounted to an easel back with chrome-plated, embossed steel bands. Size: 2¹¹⁄₁₆ X 3⁷⁄₁₆". Window: 1⁷⁄₁₆ X 1⅞". Photo: Bob Nolan.

Left:
Circa 1940. "To My Pal" greeting frame. Streamlined design silk-screened in cherry red and ivory, accented with silver mirroring, on ⅛"-thick glass. Mounted to an easel back with embossed steel bands. Size: 2⅝ X 3⅜". Window: 1⁵⁄₁₆ X 1¾". Photo: Bing Crosby.

Greetings

Many frames produced during the 1930s and 1940s included a short, often sentimental message silk-screened on the glass face as an integral part of the overall design. Messages such as "To My Pal" or "Always Yours" grace these frames, which were usually smaller in size and designed to hold a snapshot. Seasonal themes were also addressed on this type of frame, marketed for use as a holiday gift or in place of a standard greeting card.

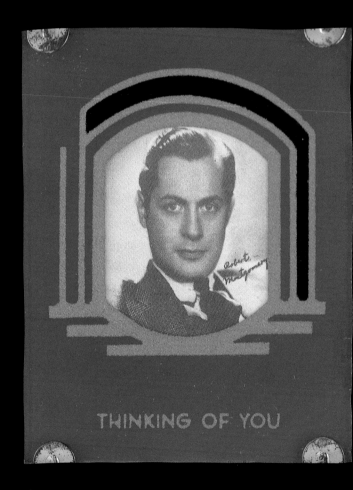

Above:
Circa 1935. "Thinking of You" greeting frame. Moderne design silk-screened in magenta, metallic gold, and black on 1/8"-thick glass. Mounted to an easel back with embossed aluminum bands.
Size: 2³⁄₄ x 3¹⁄₂".
Window: 1³⁄₈ x 1⁵⁄₈".
Photo: Robert Montgomery.

Below:
Circa 1934. "Thinking of You" greeting frame. Rope and anchor design silk-screened in ivory, black, and metallic silver on 1/8"-thick glass. Mounted to an easel back with embossed steel bands. Size: 2⁷/₁₆ x 3¹/₂". Heart-shaped window: 1⁹/₁₆ x 1⁵/₈". Photo: Fred Astaire.

Below:
Circa 1936. "Always Thinking of You" greeting frame. Horseshoe design silk-screened in black and forest green, accented with silver mirroring, on 1/8"-thick glass. Mounted to an easel back with embossed steel bands. Size: 2¹¹/₁₆ x 3⁷/₁₆". Window: 1⁷/₁₆ x 1⁷/₈". Photo: Fred Gilman.

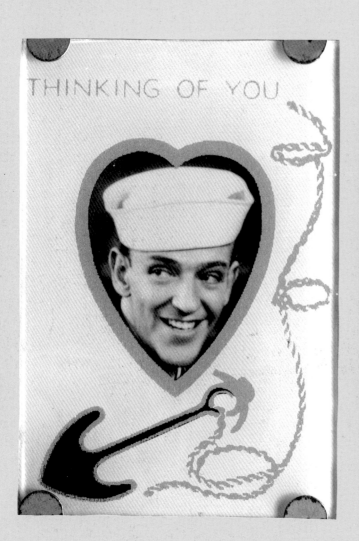

ALWAYS YOURS

Above:
Circa 1937. "Always Yours"
greeting frame. Rope and anchor
design silk-screened in black and
metallic gold on ⅛"-thick glass.
Mounted to an easel back with
nickel-plated steel bands.
Size: 2½ x 3½".
Window: 1¼ x 1½".
Photo: John Wayne.

Below:
Circa 1938. "With Love"
greeting frame. Silk-screened
in pink, black, and metallic gold
on ⅛"-thick glass. Glued to an
easel back. Size: 2½ x 3½".
Window: 1⅜ x 1¾".
Photo: Charles Starett.

Below:
Circa 1938. "With Love"
greeting frame. Silk-screened
in cornflower blue, ivory, and
metallic gold on ⅛"-thick glass.
Glued to an easel back.
Size: 2½ x 3½".
Window: 1⅜ x 1¾".
Photo: Roy Rogers.

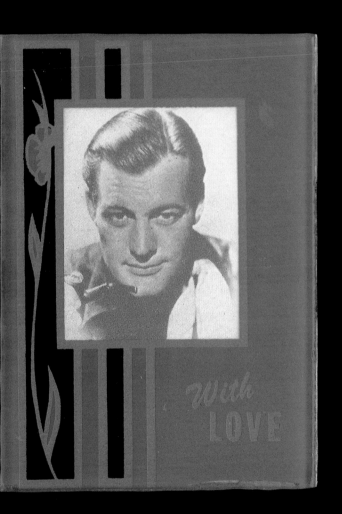

Below:
Circa 1938. "With Love"
greeting frame. Silk-screened
in sea-foam green, ivory, and
metallic gold on ⅛"-thick glass.
Glued to an easel back.
Size: 2½ x 3½".
Window: 1⅜ x 1¾".
Photo: Larry "Buster" Crabbe.

Below:
Circa 1938. "With Love"
greeting frame. Silk-screened
in beige, black, and metallic
gold on ⅛"-thick glass. Glued to
an easel back. Size: 2½ x 3½".
Window: 1⅜ x 1¾".
Photo: Edmund Cobb.

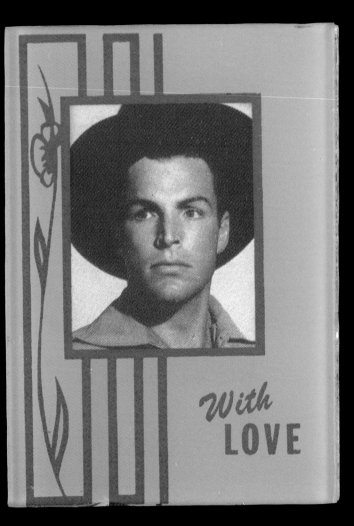

Below:
Circa 1930. Advertising
greeting frame. Geometric
design silk-screened in black
and dark teal on $\frac{1}{8}$"-thick glass,
with clear areas backed by a
silver foil mat. Held on an easel
back by a framing of $\frac{3}{16}$"-wide
black lacquered steel.
Size: $3\frac{5}{16}$ x $5\frac{5}{16}$".
Window: $2\frac{13}{16}$ x $1\frac{5}{8}$".
Photo: Bette Davis.

150

Below:
Circa 1930. "Thinking of You" greeting frame. Silk-screened in sand, black, and metallic gold on ⅛"-thick glass. Mounted to an easel back with nickel-plated steel bands. Size: 3⁷⁄₁₆ X 5½". Rare double windows: 1³⁄₈ X 1¾". Photos: Oliver Hardy and Stan Laurel.

Overleaf left:
Circa 1941. "Holiday Greetings" frame. Bell and reindeer design silk-screened in holly green, poinsettia red, gray, and metallic gold on ⅛"-thick glass. Mounted to an easel back with embossed steel bands. Size: 4 x 5".
Window: 2 x 2⁷⁄₁₆".
Photo: Lana Turner.

Overleaf right:
Circa 1941. "Merry Christmas" greeting frame. Poinsettia and holly design silk-screened in green, red, and metallic gold on ⅛"-thick glass. Mounted to an easel back with embossed steel bands. Size: 4 x 5".
Window: 2 x 2⁷⁄₁₆".
Photo: Hedy LaMarr.

Lana Turner

HOLIDAY Greetings

Selected Bibliography

Battersby, Martin. *The Decorative Thirties.* New York: Walker & Company, 1971.

———. *The Decorative Twenties.* New York: Walker & Company, 1969.

Bayer, Patricia. *Art Deco Source Book.* Secaucus, NJ: Wellfleet Press, 1988.

Blum, Daniel. *A Pictorial History of the Silent Screen.* New York: Grosset & Dunlap, 1953.

Bull, Clarence Sinclair. *The Faces of Hollywood.* Cranberry, NJ: A.S. Barnes & Company, Inc., 1968.

Burns, J.T. *Framing Pictures.* New York: Charles Scribner's Sons, 1978.

Bush, Donald J. *The Streamlined Decade.* New York: George Braziller, 1975.

Eames, John Douglas. *MGM Story.* New York: Crown Publishing, 1975.

Ford, Colin, ed. *The Story of Popular Photography.* New York: Trafalgar Square Publishing, 1989.

Franklin, Joe. *Classics of the Silent Screen.* New York: Citadel Press, 1959.

Glass Center/New York World's Fair. *The Miracle of Glass.* New York: Glass Incorporated, 1939.

Greif, Martin. *Depression Modern: The Thirties Style in America.* New York: Universe Books, 1975.

Griffith, Richard. *The Movie Stars.* Garden City, NY: Doubleday, 1970.

Henry Ford Museum and Greenfield Village. *Streamlining America: A Henry Ford Museum Exhibit.* Dearborn, MI: Henry Ford Museum, 1986.

Hillier Bevis. *Art Deco of the 20's and 30's.* New York: E.P. Dutton, 1968.

———. *The World of Art Deco.* New York: Alfred A. Knopf, 1986.

Hine, Thomas. *Populuxe.* New York: Alfred A. Knopf, 1986.

Horsham, Michael. *20's and 30's Style.* Secaucus, NJ: Wellfleet Press, 1988.

Jenkins, Alan. *The Twenties.* New York: Universe Books, 1974.

Katz, Sylvia. *Plastics: Common Objects, Classic Designs.* New York: Harry N. Abrams, 1984.

Klein, Dan. *Art Deco.* London: Treasure Press, 1984.

Lesieture, Alain. *The Spirit and Splendour of Art Deco.* New York: Paddington Press, 1974.

Maryanski, Richard A. *Antique Picture Frame Guide.* Cedar Forest Company, 1973.

Meikle, Jeffrey L. *Twentieth Century Limited: Industrial Design in America, 1925-1939.* Philadelphia: Temple University Press, 1979.

Menten, Theodore. *The Art Deco Style.* New York: Dover Publications, 1972.

Robinson, Julian. *The Golden Age of Style.* New York: Harcourt Brace & Jovanovich, 1976.

Weber, Eva. *Art Deco in America.* New York: Exeter Books, 1985.

Above:
Circa 1939, Moderne-style frame silk-screened in green, accented with hand-engraved lines painted in metallic gold, on ⅛"-thick glass. Mounted to an easel back by hammered brass rosettes, accented with brass backplates.
Size: 10 x 12".
Window: 6¾ x 8¾".
Photo: Barbara Stanwyck.

Above:
Circa 1940, Moderne-style frame silk-screened in blue and ivory on ⅛"-thick glass. Held on an easel back by a framing of ¼"-wide painted pine. Size: 10³⁄₁₆ x 12¼".
Window: 7³⁄₁₆ x 9³⁄₁₆".
Photo: Kenny Baker.

Photo Index

Portraits of movie stars appear on page numbers listed.

Above:
Circa 1935, Moderne-style frame
silk-screened in beige, black, and
metallic gold on 1/8"-thick glass.
Glued to an easel back.
Size: 2½ x 3½".
Window: 1⅜ x 1¾".
Photo: Buck Jones.

Acknowledgments

Robert Alder, Peacock
  Laboratories, Philadelphia.
Don Ameche, Los Angeles.
Lew Ayres, Los Angeles.
Mary Baber, Olsson-Baber
  Photography Studio,
  Chicago.
Jack Baldus and Jac-Kard
  Designs, Chicago.
Eastman Kodak Company,
  Rochester, NY.
Marsha Evaskus, Zig-Zag
  Antiques, Chicago.
Douglas Fairbanks, Jr.,
  New York.
Nancy Gabler, Chicago.
Linda Gannon, Chicago.
Genou, Chicago.
Granville Gallery, Chicago.
Adrienne (Starr) Ingebrigtsen,
  Indian Head Park, Illinois.
Abbie Jacobson, Chicago.
Robert Janjigian, Rizzoli,
  New York.
Linda LeSage, New York.
Claudia Menza, New York.
Metropolitan Home,
  New York.
Jeffrey Najoum, Chicago.
Stanley Paul, Chicago.
Pioneer Glass, Chicago.
Lt.Col.Pritchett and Cpt.
  Deeter, Camp Robinson,
  North Little Rock, AK
Gilbert Roland, Beverly Hills.
Cesar Romero, Los Angeles.
Ann Sothern, Ketchum, ID.
Gloria Starr, Chicago.
Jimmy Stewart, Los Angeles.
Gloria Stuart, Los Angeles.
Jean E, Verlich, PPG Industries,
  Inc., Pittsburgh.
Roberta (Starr) Weiss, Morland
  Hills, Ohio.
Yesterday, Chicago.
Robert Young, Westlake
  Village, CA.